When We Are Sick

Staying Healthy

You can get sick.

Your family can get sick.

Your friends can get sick.

Look at my dad.

I can help him,

when he is sick.

My mom will help me,
when I am sick.

11

Look at the doctor.

The doctor will help us,
when we are sick.

Look at the nurse.
The nurse will help us,
when we are sick.

15

These people can help me, when I am sick.